CLOSER LOOK A..

MW00908441

THE RAINFOREST

Selina Wood

STARGAZER BOOKS

New edition published in 2005

Designed and produced by
Aladdin Books Ltd

First paperback edition published in the United States
in 2005 by
Stargazer Books
c/o The Creative Company
123 South Broad Street
P.O. Box 227
Mankato, Minnesota 56002

Editor
Alex Edmonds

Designer
Gary Edgar-Hyde

Picture Research
Brooks Krikler Research

Illustrators
James Macdonald
Ian Moores
John Lobban – B.L. Kearley Ltd.
Richard Orr
David Burroughs
Ron Hayward Associates and Aziz H. Khan

Certain illustrations have appeared in
earlier books created by Aladdin Books

Printed in U.A.E.

Cataloging-in-Publication data is available from the
Library of Congress.
ISBN: 1-932799-87-7

CONTENTS

INTRODUCTION

The tropical rainforests are probably teeming with more plants and animals than any other habitat on Earth. They are one of the world's most valuable resources, yet humankind carelessly clears the forests, destroying people's homes, potential food and medicine, and the habitats of many plants and animals. Since the mid-1980s the fate of the tropical rainforests has caused widespread concern; and the race is on to save them.

Life at the top

The branches of the highest trees form a canopy as high as 164 feet above the ground. Above this rise a few taller trees known as emergents. Shorter trees form a lower layer, called the sub-canopy, 66 feet high.

The tallest trees are called emergents

Canopy

Sub-Canopy

Where old trees die, new ones sprout and take 75-100 years to grow to full height

Undergrowth

Thick buttress roots hold up the tall trees

A thin layer of soil is useless for agriculture

Tropical rainforests grow in regions with a climate that is constantly wet and hot. These conditions have caused the rainforests to evolve over millions of years into one of the most complex ecosystems on Earth. It is the trees that dominate the rainforests. From the sky the forest looks like a huge green carpet, covering thousands of miles.

WHAT IS A

INSIDE THE FOREST

The rainforest has a huge number of tree species. You could walk through the forest for an hour and not see the same species of tree twice. Deep in the rainforest it is humid and very hot. Even in the daytime it is still and dark. Animals are most active and noisy at night, but their camouflage hides them in the dense foliage.

Characteristic of most rainforests are buttress roots (which extend down from the tree trunks) and climbing plants (see right), both of which help to support the tall trees.

ON CLOSER INSPECTION – *Mangrove*

Mangrove is a type of rainforest found near coastal waters. It can be seen in the Everglades in Florida, where it is home to both alligators and sea cows. The stilt roots of the mangrove trees take in water but filter out the salt, which is toxic to most trees.

RAINFOREST?

RAINFOREST THE RECYCLER

Everything is recycled very quickly in the rainforest. When it rains, the roots of the trees take in water. This water travels up the tree and into the leaves. From there it is slowly released into the air, forming rain clouds. Rain from these clouds will then fall over other parts of the forest. Dead plants and animals also have a part to play in the recycling. They decay quickly in the hot, humid conditions. Their nutrients are then taken up by plant and tree roots or washed down out of the soil by rainwater. This leaves a thin soil that is not very fertile.

Water passes back into the air through leaves of vegetation

Sun

Rainfall

Vegetation takes in water

Tree frog

Thin soil layer

Groundwater

River

Water evaporates from river by sun's heat

River runs to the sea

Amazonia
The largest area of tropical forests in the world is among the vast Amazonian river basin. Tributaries (above) stretch as far as Brazil, Venezuela, Colombia, and Peru.

Africa
In Africa, the forest is mainly found around the Zaire river basin (below). Some areas of the African rainforest are thought to be over 60 million years old.

Tropical rainforests mostly grow around the Equator, where it is hot all year (68-95° F) and it rains heavily every day (there are 60-80 inches of rain per year). This area is called the tropics. Rainforests are found in Latin America, western Africa, and Southeast Asia. Most are in developing countries where people rely on the forests for their food and shelter.

WHERE ARE

RAINFORESTS BEFORE...
Before deforestation (see page 12) became such a problem, rainforests covered huge areas of Africa, South and Central America, Asia, and the Pacific Islands. Tropical rainforests from different parts of the world may have similar features, such as heavy rainfall and hot, humid conditions, but there are variations between the plant and animal life in these areas. For example, three snakes, all living in the rainforest – the bushmaster snake from South America, the black mamba from Africa, and the krait from Asia – come from the same family, the *Elapidae*, but they don't look at all similar.

South America

ON CLOSER INSPECTION
– Temperate rainforest?

There are some rainforests outside the tropics. In lands that are temperate (have moderate climates), but where there is plenty of rain and the weather is mild, rainforests can thrive. This one (right) is in Victoria, in southeast Australia.

THEY?

Asia

In eastern Asia the rainforest zone extends from southern China to northern Australia, and includes the Indo-Pacific Islands. There is also a narrow rainforest zone along the west coast of India. Now many forests, like this one in Indonesia, are disappearing fast.

Current extent of tropical rainforests (green)

Previous extent of tropical rainforests (yellow)

Africa

Equator

Indian Ocean

Australia

Madagascar

Photosynthesis

Plants in the rainforest get a lot of light energy from the sun to grow, because of the hot climate. This process is called photosynthesis. Water and CO_2 are changed into sugar foods for the plant.

Oxygen produced

Sunlight gives energy for growth

CO_2 enters leaves from the air

Sugar is formed

Water and minerals combine with CO_2

The rainforests contain over half of the world's known plant and animal species, but cover only 11% of the land surface. A variety of creatures live in the forests – from the forest floor right up to the canopy. Scientists are sure that there are still many more species to be discovered

TEEMING

Fungi eat into fallen branches and twigs

Insects crunch up dead plant material

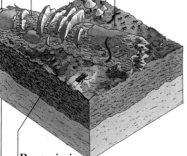

Bacteria in the soil break down everything that remains

Decomposition

Dead animal and vegetable matter is rapidly broken down and washed into the soil. Here its minerals are reabsorbed through the roots of the trees.

THE LIVING FOREST

High in the canopy live brightly colored birds, like toucans and macaws, with a few mammals, such as the squirrel monkey. Below, in the understory, large mammals like gorillas and leopards make their homes. Only plants that like the shade can survive on the dark, warm, forest floor. Many, like the bromeliad, have specially shaped leaves that take in water directly from the very damp air. The floor of the forest is covered in fallen leaves, mosses, and fungi. Millions of insects live here among the plants.

Oleander hawk moth

Hercules beetle

Bromeliad

Noctuid moth

Leaf long horned grass-hopper

Ants

Lichen

Ant spider

Orange orchid Maxilleria

ON CLOSER INSPECTION
– Convergent evolution

Hornbills of Africa and toucans of the South American rainforests come from different continents, but they have grown to look alike because they have such similar lives in similar habitats. This is an example of what scientists call convergent evolution.

Toucan

Hornbill

WITH LIFE

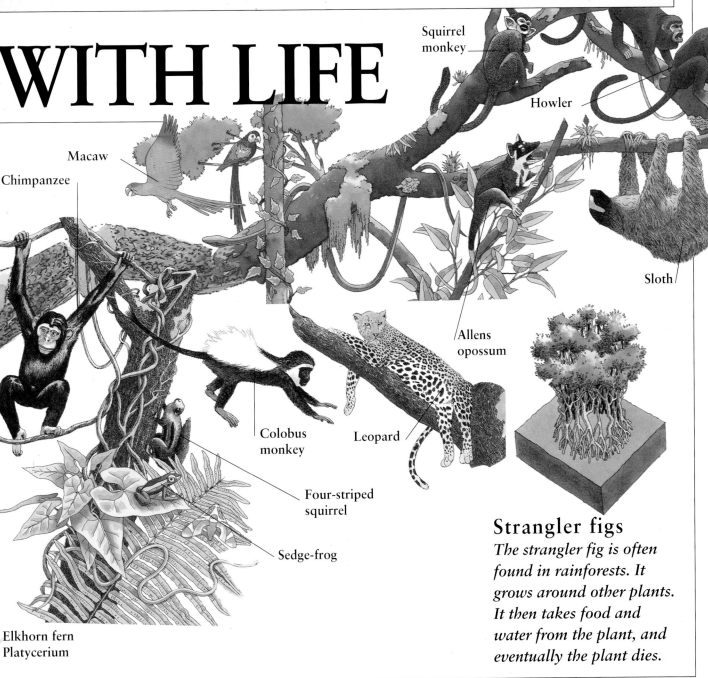

Squirrel monkey

Howler

Macaw

Chimpanzee

Sloth

Allens opossum

Colobus monkey

Leopard

Four-striped squirrel

Sedge-frog

Elkhorn fern
Platycerium

Strangler figs
The strangler fig is often found in rainforests. It grows around other plants. It then takes food and water from the plant, and eventually the plant dies.

Rainforests cover only a fraction of the area they did in the past because they have been destroyed by humans. Every day large areas of forest disappear as trees are felled, bulldozed, or burned down. No one is sure of the exact rate of worldwide deforestation, but it could be as much as 87,000 miles^2 per yea

GOING,

Deforestation

The destruction of forests by humans is called "deforestation." It is taking place at such a rate that forests do not have a chance to grow back. True rainforests, with their huge range of species, took millions of years to evolve.

A SPEEDY END

Tropical rainforest destruction started in earnest about 500 years ago, when the demand for tropical produce, such as wood, first started. The pace has quickened since the beginning of the twentieth century, with the introduction of the chainsaw and an increase in demand for rainforest produce. As a result, since 1950 nearly half of the rainforests that existed at the turn of the century have disappeared.

Chart showing a selection of predicted annual deforestation rates based on 1990 figures.	
Brazil (South America)	25,000 miles^2 (40,000 km^2)
Indonesia (Southeast Asia)	7,000 miles^2 (11,000 km^2)
Zaire (Africa)	4,300 miles^2 (7,000 km^2)
Venezuela (South America)	3,400 miles^2 (5,500 km^2)
Thailand (Southeast Asia)	23,000 miles^2 (37,000 km^2)
Ivory Coast (Africa)	621 miles^2 (1,000 km^2)

In both Thailand and Brazil a huge area of trees, bigger than the size of Belgium, is destroyed each year.

ON CLOSER INSPECTION
– *Hotspot*

Brazil (right) is the biggest deforester, accounting for about 28% of world tropical rainforest destruction. Even in the 16th century, in Brazil, rainforests were cleared to grow crops and build homes for foreign settlers.

GOING, GONE...

DIFFERENT SPEEDS

Rates of forest destruction vary throughout the world. For instance, Venezuelan forest is not experiencing much clearance at the moment, but at the end of the 1980s, over 80% of the forest had been cleared in Nigeria. And in Madagascar, off the coast of Africa, the forests are now in danger of disappearing completely (below).

SATELLITE

Deforestation rates are hard to assess because the areas of land are so vast and there is a lack of data – because there is no set method of calculating it. The most accurate way is using satellite pictures (above). But this method is expensive, and some satellites can only detect deforestation caused by fire.

There are many reasons why the rainforests are being cleared, but the main ones are money and survival. Some people cut down the forests to make large profits from the raw materials. Many areas are also cleared by people who are forced to grow crops on forest land because there is nowhere else for them to go.

WHY IS IT

Uganda
In certain areas around Uganda, in Africa (above), plantation agriculture is common. This means that specialized crops such as cacoa are grown in huge quantities, specifically for selling abroad. Clearance of forests is necessary for this to be possible. As a result, hundreds of families are left homeless, as large areas of trees are felled to make way for the crops.

Threats to the rainforest

ROAD TO DISASTER
The destructive impact on the forest increases as more people move into it. Roads are built through remote areas to improve transportation and for loggers to exploit new areas of timber. People looking for land to live off follow these roads to cultivate new areas of land. Eventually they move on to another new patch. This method of farming, called "shifted cultivation," destroys surrounding forest and saps the nutrients from the soil so that it cannot grow back.

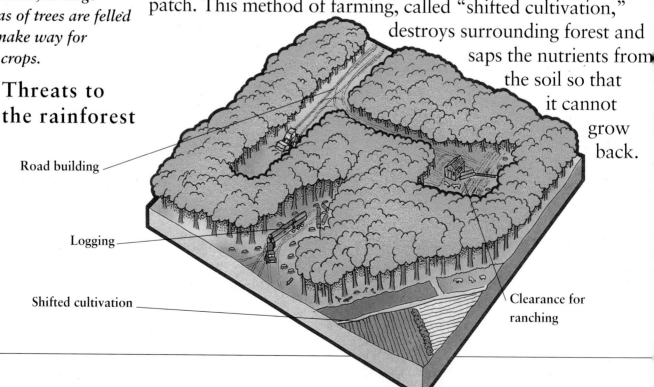

Road building

Logging

Shifted cultivation

Clearance for ranching

On Closer Inspection
– *A better life?*

To combat overcrowding in cities, governments encourage people to move to forest areas. Many of these settlers do not know which crops are best for forest soils. When crop yields are poor, they then have to move on to other areas, where more trees are felled (right).

HAPPENING?

TIMBERRRR!

Many trees are logged to provide timber to sell abroad. Quick profits can be made from logging (left), but it causes enormous destruction. This is not only because of the trees felled, but also, indirectly, because nearby trees are damaged by machinery, as is the wildlife. The collection of firewood by people living near the forest (left) is another cause of clearance, in Africa particularly. Often it is the only source of fuel people have for cooking and heat.

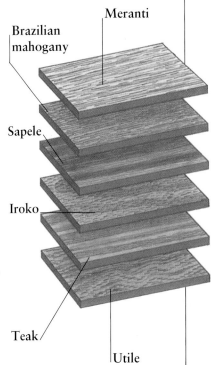

Meranti

Brazilian mahogany

Sapele

Iroko

Teak

Utile

Tropical woods
Rainforest woods are very hard-wearing. They are used as luxury woods and building timber. Teak and mahogany are usually used to make good quality, often expensive, furniture.

Dam pests!

Dams can cause problems. A build-up of silt causes rapid growth of algal plant life, which can kill fish. Also stagnant water, found in the reservoirs, provides an excellent breeding ground for mosquitoes carrying malaria (below).

S ome rainforests, particularly those in Amazonia, are being cleared by governments to make way for large scale development projects. They include dams for hydroelectricity and mining for the rich mineral stores underneath the rainforest. The aim is to create wealth, but eventually the opposite may occur.

DAMS AND

DAM DESTRUCTION

Dams are often built in the well-watered rainforest river valleys to produce hydroelectric power. Channels inside the dams allow some of the water to escape through turbines. The fast-flowing water rotates turbines, which power electricity generators. Before a dam, such as the Tucurui dam (right), is built, people and animals have to be cleared from the area. If trees are left to rot underwater, rather than felled, they acidify the water, and this eats away at the machinery inside the dam.

On Closer Inspection
– *A new profession*

When the Tucurui dam in Brazil was built, trees were not cleared before the reservoir was filled. As a result "scuba lumberjacks" had to log trees underwater (right). The cut wood floats to the surface, where it can easily be moved away, making it a less expensive process.

MINES

GOLD RUSH!

The Amazon basin contains enormous mineral and oil wealth, as do parts of New Guinea, the Philippines, and Indonesia. Although mining is not a direct threat to the rainforests, it brings new roads and increased development that attracts settlers. Illegal gold mining by itinerant peoples in Amazonia (below) has resulted in the pollution of rivers and the disturbance of local tribal peoples.

Product demand

It is the wealthy countries that create the demand for rainforest products, such as timber. Four-fifths of the hardwood is exported to developed countries and used in luxury furniture and construction. These same countries have invested a lot of money in helping some rainforest countries, such as Brazil.

D espite the rainforest's rich and varied plant and animal life, it is quite fragile. Plants and animals depend on each other and on a healthy and unchanging habitat for survival. The disturbance of just a small area of forest can spell disaster for thousands of species by destroying their habitats. Many of them are becoming extinct.

Rhino trouble

There may be millions of animals, insects, and plants, still unknown, that could become extinct without us ever discovering them. Other animals that we have all seen in zoos or in picture books are also at risk. An example of this is the West Bengal rhinoceros (above) which may become extinct soon.

PARADISE

EFFECTS OF HABITAT LOSS

Some scientists think that as many as 50 rainforest species are becoming extinct every day. Below are a few of the species in danger. Animals and plants are affected by the clearing of the forests in a number of ways. They can die in forest fires or suffer from the loss of habitat. Even the logging of a few selected trees creates stress for animals if their home or food supply is destroyed. Habitat loss means a shrinking area in which to live and increased competition for food in the remaining area.

Indri
Madagascar

Aye-aye
Madagascar

Manatee
Amazon

Jentik's duiker
West Africa

ON CLOSER INSPECTION
– So long, tiger!

Tigers are one of the few species found only in the rainforest, but they are under threat from extinction. At the turn of the century there were more than 40,000 tigers in India alone. Now there are only about 3,750 left, and that number is shrinking.

LOST

Monkey-eating eagle
Philippines

Dove langur
South Asia

GORILLA GAP

The mountain gorilla (below), which lives in the rainforests of Africa, is very rare – there are only 650 of them left in the world. In Rwanda and Uganda they are under threat in many ways. They are killed for food, their skull and hands are sold as souvenirs, and they are shot as an agricultural pest. In addition, their forest habitat is being destroyed. Some gorillas are protected in National Parks, but more needs to be done to ensure their survival.

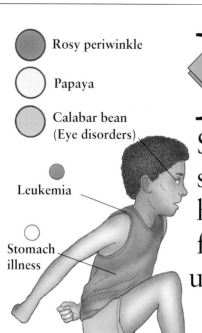

Rosy periwinkle

Papaya

Calabar bean
(Eye disorders)

Leukemia

Stomach
illness

Rainforests already provide many riches in the form of foods, medicines, and raw materials. Scientists believe that so far only 1% of species that could exist in the rainforest have been discovered. If destruction of forest habitats continues, the remaining undiscovered species could be lost forever.

DOCTOR

Doctor's chart
The following rainforest plants can be used to make medicines: the rosy periwinkle of Madagascar for leukemia; the calabar bean of West Africa for eye disorders; and the papaya of Latin America for stomach complaints.

Tea Sugar Spices Lemons

Coffee Cocoa

Brazil nuts

Oranges

Rice

Avocados Bananas

Beans

FOREST MENU
Many of the world's foodstuffs, including coffee, tea, tomatoes, bananas, pineapples, avocados, corn, cocoa, rice, and chilies originate from tropical forests. Though most of these plants are now grown on plantations, wild plants are vital for providing genetic diversity (keeping different varieties of the various species).

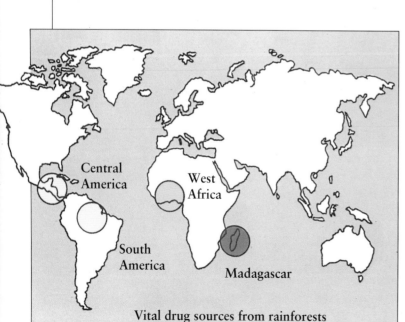

Central America

West Africa

South America

Madagascar

Vital drug sources from rainforests

ON CLOSER INSPECTION
– *Poison arrows*

The Amazonian Indians (right) use a poison, known as *curare,* on their hunting arrows. The *curare* paralyzes the animal by stopping its muscles from working. It is now adapted and used to relax patients' muscles before surgery.

RAINFOREST

MEDICAL CHEST

At least a quarter of the world's medicines are based on rainforest plants. They include antibiotics, painkillers, tranquilizers, and cancer-fighting drugs. Some scientists think that as many as 10% of the plants that haven't been tested yet might be used to fight cancer, and that among the rainforest plants one could even hold the cure for AIDS.

A LOT TO LEARN

Traditional village healers (left) know all about the rainforest. They use hundreds of different seeds, fruits, flowers, and roots from the forest to treat people. If these people are driven from their homes and their knowledge is lost, we will also lose the key to making most of these products.

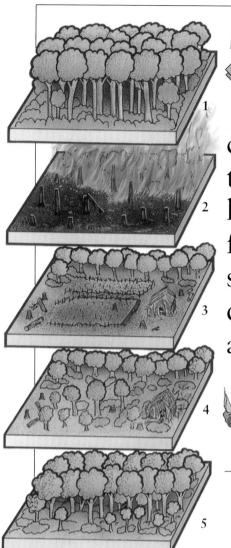

The most direct impact of deforestation is on the forest peoples. In seventy tropical countries across the world, millions of tribal people rely on the rainforest. They have lived in harmony with the forest for thousands of years, getting food and shelter from it without destroying or damaging it. These are the people who are at risk from forest clearance.

FOREST

Yams

Sweet peppers

Cassavas

Okra pods

Chilies

Shifting cultivation

Many forest people clear patches of forest to grow crops, but do no lasting damage. They choose a small area of forest (1), clear and burn it (2), grow crops that don't take all of the nutrients from the soil (3), continue to grow different crops over a few years (4), farm the land carefully and not intensively (5), then leave the forest to grow back.

ON CLOSER INSPECTION
– *Tribal meeting*

In 1989 the Kayapó tribe organized the first meeting of Brazilian Indian tribes to protest against a planned government dam scheme that would leave them homeless (right). It was successful because funds for the scheme were withdrawn, which prevented it from going ahead.

PEOPLES

BROKEN HOMES

Since settlers have started to move into and demolish the rainforests, the native peoples have suffered badly. Their forest homes have been destroyed. They have died from diseases brought in by settlers from outside, such as chickenpox. They have also been forced to move out of the forests into new environments to which they are not suited.

TRIBES

There are about 1,000 rainforest tribes around the world. The territory of the Kayapó tribe in the Amazon (below) has been invaded many times since the 18th century. Eighty-five percent of the tribe died after their first contact with settlers carrying Western diseases.

T ropical rainforest destruction affects the natural environment greatly. It leaves land prone to soil erosion, which causes floods and droughts in local areas. It also disrupts local weather conditions, which in turn affect global weather patterns.

Global warming

All plants absorb carbon dioxide (CO$_2$), using it to grow. When trees and plants are burned, they release CO$_2$ back into the air. CO$_2$ and certain other "greenhouse gases" trap the sun's heat as it is reflected back from Earth, creating the "greenhouse effect." This heat is essential for life, but if the greenhouse effect increases, due to more gases in the air (caused by large-scale forest burning), the Earth's climate may change by becoming warmer.

WATER CYCLE

The rainforests affect rainfall. Clouds form above the forest from moisture given off by the leaves. The rain that falls is reabsorbed by the trees. If a forest is cleared, there are no tree roots to prevent the soil and water from escaping. Heavy rain and winds blow the soil away, leaving ground unprotected.

A WORLD

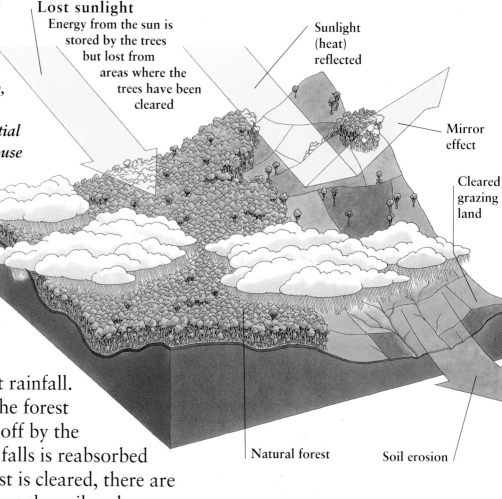

Lost sunlight
Energy from the sun is stored by the trees but lost from areas where the trees have been cleared

Sunlight (heat) reflected

Mirror effect

Cleared grazing land

Natural forest

Soil erosion

A rainforest is like a giant sponge: Water is soaked up by the trees and by the plants that live on them.

ON CLOSER INSPECTION
– *Brazil nuts*

Brazil-nut trees are protected by law because of their commercial value. Strangely, if a rainforest area has been cleared, the Brazil-nut tree cannot produce nuts – it needs the surrounding forest to flourish.

OF DIFFERENCE

FLOODS AND DROUGHTS

When rainforest trees are removed, what is left behind is bare earth. In hilly areas this means that large amounts of water run off the land instead of being trapped by the forests, so soil is washed away and floods occur. Flooding in the Philippines (right) is a typical example of this.

FLOODED FOREST

Although some rainforests experience natural seasonal floods, deforestation and the building of dams cause excessive regional flooding, which is harmful. The picture on the left shows conservationists trying to record and preserve plant species after the building of a dam in Guyana had drowned many species.

S aving the rainforests is a very complicated problem. Rainforest countries, frequently plagued by poverty and rapidly expanding populations, are under pressure to make use of the forest resources. International organizations have been striving to protect the forests, while allowing some development that can be continued with the minimum of destruction.

National parks

One way of protecting nature is to turn areas into nature reserves (above). In 1990 there were about 560 tropical forest parks covering about 4% of all tropical forests, but more are needed. These parks preserve species diversity.

Ways forward

Efforts to save the forests have involved "reforestation" and "sustainable harvesting" of the forest. Reforestation (planting more trees) cannot recreate natural rainforest conditions, but can help to restore CO_2 levels in the atmosphere. "Sustainable" development gives protection to the forests while allowing some development that can be continued in the future. An example of this is the logging of commercially valuable trees, while leaving surrounding trees undisturbed. But this is very difficult to control. Special areas for planting trees that are commercially valuable (plantations) may also take pressure off the rainforests.

WHAT HAS

Protected forests
In some countries, small sections of forest are protected, which means they cannot be cut down

Reforestation
Growing new trees can be difficult because rainforest soil is not very rich

Jungle patrols
Where new trees are planted, special "jungle police" protect them from being cut down

ON CLOSER INSPECTION
– *Non-timber profits*

Changing from the production of wood to non-wood products helps save trees and is also profitable. Rubber (latex) is a traditional rainforest product and was one of the first to be harvested without pulling any trees down (right). If managed carefully, it causes no harm to the forest at all.

BEEN DONE?

Environmental conference at the June, 1992 Earth Summit in Rio de Janeiro, Brazil

INTERNATIONAL ACTION

Since the 1980s the Tropical Forestry Action Plan has worked to restore, conserve, and manage forests to benefit local people and the economy of the country concerned. The International Tropical Timber Agreement encourages cooperation between countries that produce timber and those that buy it. At the Earth Summit in Brazil in 1992 (left), several rainforest countries agreed to continue to implement "sustainable" forestry projects.

The fate of the rainforests relies on international cooperation and the education of people all over the world about the value of the rainforests. It may also depend on a fair distribution of land so that the rainforest people are not forced to cut down trees to stay alive. Certainly, if the current rates of destruction are not slowed down, the global consequences could be disastrous.

Behind bars
If the rainforests disappear, some of the Earth's most beautiful and exotic animals may only exist in zoos and in confined and unnatural reservations.

THE FUTURE

FOREST EDUCATION

Some people believe that if local people had more control over their own forest areas, their future would be more stable. Some projects have involved the education of local people in forest management. This photograph (left) shows a project worker planting trees to bind the soil, which gives long-term protection of the land. The variety of tree she is planting grows very well in this soil without removing all the nutrients from the soil.

ON CLOSER INSPECTION
– *Orangutan future*

Developing the tourist industry in rainforest countries is another way of taking pressure off rainforest products as the only source of income. People flock to see orphaned orangutans in reserves in Indonesia, and this is boosting the tourist trade and bringing in money to that area.

NATURE SWAP

Many rainforest countries have huge international debts, owed to developed countries in return for help with dam, mine, and road building. This leads to more logging of forests for quick profits to pay back their debts. One short-term solution to this is called the "debt for nature" swap. This allows developing countries to pay back some of their debts by protecting agreed-upon areas of rainforest. Another option is to stop interest payments on debts, or even cancel the debts completely. This can, and has, helped many rainforest countries to protect their land for the future.

FRIENDS *of the*
earth

Panda device © 1986 WWF – World
Wide Fund For Nature
(formerly World Wildlife Fund)
Registered ownership: ® WWF
Registered Trademark owner

GET INFORMED

Read all you can about the rainforests. Get your information from environmental groups such as World Wide Fund For Nature and Friends of the Earth, as well as from newspapers and magazines.

WHAT CAN YOU DO?

EXOTIC PLANTS AND PETS

If you buy an exotic plant or animal, like an orchid or parrot (below), check that it is not an endangered species and it has not been collected in the wild at the risk of extinction. Many species are smuggled in terrible conditions and die on the journey.

WOOD CONTROL

Encourage your friends and family to use paper-recycling bins. Ask suppliers to order wood from sources certified through the Forest Stewardship Council. They check that the wood is from producers who manage rainforest areas sensibly, without harming forests.

TO SUM IT ALL UP...

The whole world benefits from the rainforests, so we should not leave it up to governments and environmental groups to save them. Above are some of the things that we can do to make a difference. Remember that there is still much work to be done before the fate of the Earth's disappearing paradise is secure!

GLOSSARY

Canopy The top layer of the rainforest. It is like the forest's roof, and is made up of the tops of the very tall trees. It makes first contact with sunlight and rain.

Equator An invisible circle around the center of the Earth, dividing the North and South Hemispheres.

Generator A device to turn mechanical energy into electrical energy.

Global warming A gradual increase in temperatures across the world, possibly caused by more heat being trapped in the atmosphere by greenhouse gases.

Greenhouse effect The warming effect created when the sun's heat is reflected back from the Earth's surface and trapped by certain gases in the atmosphere.

Greenhouse gas A gas in the atmosphere that adds to the greenhouse effect.

Habitat The natural home of a plant or animal.

Humidity Air quality that is very moist and damp.

Photosynthesis The method plants use to convert the sun's energy into sugars for growth.

Plantation farming A type of farming practiced in some rainforest countries, which is designed to supply the needs of foreign markets. It usually involves growing just one crop in huge quantities.

Rainforest A forest that grows where it is warm and rainy throughout the year.

Ranching A type of farming where large areas of land are grazed by big herds of cattle. Many areas of rainforest have been cleared for cattle ranching. The cattle are bred for meat and milk.

Resources Sources of energy and raw materials found in and around the Earth.

Shifted cultivation A kind of farming where people have been shifted into the forest because they are poor; there is nowhere else for them to go. They clear an area of forest, burn the trees, and then grow crops. The forest then cannot recover because all of the nutrients have been used up.

Shifting cultivation The farming carried out by native peoples that does not harm the rainforest. The people clear only small areas of land, and they grow crops that belong in the rainforest. They move on before the land is exhausted and the forest recovers.

Silt A fine deposit of mud, clay, or other substances that are found in a river.

"Sustainable" development Development programs designed to be easy to continue after a period of training.

Turbine A machine with rotating blades that converts the energy from a moving liquid or gas into another form of energy, such as electricity.

INDEX

Photo credits

Abbreviations: t-top, m-middle, b-bottom, r-right, l-left. All pictures in this book are supplied by Frank Spooner Pictures, apart from the following pages:-7, 18, & 21m - Eye Ubiquitous. 9t - Bruce Coleman Collection. 14 & 17t - Panos pictures. 30t - Panda Device © 1986 WWF - World Wide Fund for Nature (formerly World Wildlife Fund) WWF ® Registered trademark owner. 30 tr - courtesy of Friends of the Earth.